CHANCIN
THE WEATHER

by the Londonderry Poets

Betty Hord Edelman
Bruce Hesselbach
Timothy Swaim Johnson
Virginia Love
Anne Mausolff
Anne Yarosevich

Published by Bralicon Press
Newfane, Vermont

Bralicon Press
43 Bruce Brook Road
Newfane, Vt. 05345

ISBN 0-9643016-1-x
Library of Congress Catalog Card Number
00 130112

TABLE OF CONTENTS

PREFACE

What a joy it has been to be part of this group! The Londonderry Poets were formed in 1991 by Virginia Love and Margaret Houskeeper, then residents of Londonderry, Vermont. In the early years we met in the Garden Restaurant in Londonderry, but lately most often in Chester or Andover. We produced our first book, *Blackberry Picking*, in December, 1994.

The inspiration and encouragement that comes from this group has been immeasurable. For example, for one meeting, all the six poets were asked to produce something in a foreign language. The result: poems in eight different languages, the best of which are included, with translations, in our chapter, Tower of Babble. "Veniti Cu Mine" is Romanian; "Amancer" is Spanish; "Il Trovatore" is Italian; the rest are French.

More examples abound. The reading of difficult poems by modern authors, encouraged by Betty Edelman and Virginia Love, helped give rise to our chapter, Enigmas. Fellow poets Bruce Hesselbach and Timothy Swaim Johnson have given interesting and sometimes very funny presentations on the poetry of William Blake, Lord Byron, Thomas Hardy, and Dame Edith Sitwell. Virginia Love serenaded us on the violin; and Anne Yarosevich and Anne Mausolff inspired us with a mixture of poetry and visual art.

Now it is our pleasure to share the fruits of these joyful nights with you.

2

Chancing the Weather

4

THINGS SEEN ON THE TRAIL

There's a sense of grandiose adventure

when rising up out of thick forest

suddenly the world rolls out below you:

houses and farms, counties, vast lakes,

commerce, wealth, population, everything

tiny below your feet.

The dizzying cliffs; the cooling breeze.

Sometimes when I hike I come across

pleasing surprises like a wooden

ladder up a steep climb

or a sheer slate gray water-

fall, bridal veil threads cascading

white on the dark gray jagged edges

of a perpendicular cliff.

Or in twilight two fishers

bounding across the trail startling

us and no less our dog.

Or, in darkness coming down from Katahdin

by flashlight, the noises --

we don't want to see them --

they could be skunks!

Looming up over Noonmark, the impressive mass

of Dix Mtn., gored with slides, with

a snow cloud battering its summit.

The cloud foaming at the mouth

is a wild beast held back by chain,

then lunging forward and hurling

through Noonmark's birches with snow.

It was worth chancing the weather

to see Hurricane Mtn. crowned with hoarfrost:

white balsam firs, white saplings,

mountain ash without leaves --

red berries on white branches --

icicles dangling from rock; ice on the trail

with bubbles flowing under the ice.

How many times have I reached a mountain top

and the clouds unexpectedly cleared?

On Cardigan I saw hazy lakes and valleys

and distant mountains like whales breaching

out of white foam.

It was worth a few raindrops

to see all that.

Bruce Hesselbach

GEMSTAR

I get lost in amethyst

Where my eyes wander

to the lilt of imagination.

I stand under a waterfall

and all around me are emerald leaves

dazzling with health.

Energy! Energy!

My mouth forms a smile

that is half sunlight.

Anne Yarosevich

AUTUMNAL EQUINOX

Is this the sun
  that shone upon Jane Austen?
The sun that Ereshkigal
  Queen of the Underworld
    never sees?

The sun I cannot look at
  but that daily shines upon
a thousand times a thousand shoulders.

Radiating rays relentlessly.

To feel the sun's warmth
  on the skin
is as close to the gods as
  we'll get.

Autumnal Equinox:
  the earth holding its breath
    on tiptoes
perfectly balanced for a second.

Then lumbering over pell-mell
  to catapult through other reaches.

In harmony we turn
  and continue our journey,
    the sun shining
      on the other cheek.

Timothy Swaim Johnson

GALE TANKA

Wind-blasted pennant

calligraphed with black on white

halyard ties shredded

sails from its masthead mooring:

sea change for paper birch.

Anne Mausolff

10

ERMINE COAT

Outside my window the snow is flying
Those enduring pine trees
Tall, majestic, forever green
Wear a fluffy ermine coat
Shedding in winter wind
Like one worn too long
By a rich dowager -- then given
To a thrift shop where the garment
Passes from hand to hand -- until --
At last you see her shuffling along
A bag woman wearing an old ermine coat
Outside my window the snow is flying
The emerald pines take on
A new and fluffy ermine coat

Betty Hord Edelman

11

SUNSET

Suffused coral

the color of purple breathing

Lavender blushing

Intense shimmering --

the sky travels from white

to smoldering.

My fire is stoked by this

warm beauty --

the depths of pink

like the heart of an ember.

Mosquitoes bite

awakened from the dead.

Into the vast quietness

of night slides the sky.

Anne Yarosevich

HOARY PUCCOON

Without a boot stands Hoary Puccoon
without a shoon, Cousin Blood Root.
Though lank, yet crowned with yellow
grey-haired, mellow, on the bank
young-old Hoary, dank 'neath the willow
by high noon sends out his shoot.

Brothers Puccoon, covered with hair,
thought quite a pair, never can croon.
For an aperitif, do them eschew
nor taste them as if clover leaves.
As for Blood Root, go no further
-- yellows and reds, not blue --

leitmotif of color, not of bassoon:
Hoary, Hairy and Blood Root dye.

Anne Mausolff

AT THE PRIORY

September is a month of letting go.

As the sweet moments of summer

fly through our hands like

silk scarves in a tempest.

Anne Yarosevich

FIRST STORM

The snow has come early this year,
falling like a shroud on unraked leaves
and still exposed woodpiles.

The storm has caught us unaware,
at least those of us who would dream
away the autumn days, becoming dazed
by the sight of a sunset,
of a shimmering, egg yolk sun,
slipping into the horizon
against the brilliant blue sky,
or those of us who would pick up
the most perfect autumn leaf
from the ground and
feel like falling in love with it.

I would have been ready for the snow,
yet not have beheld the splendor.

                              Virginia Love

FALLING STAR

The hour is not one I'm used to.
 So quiet I hear
  the heat in the wood stove.

I sit up in bed,
 lackadaisical.
A good view out the window
 into the stunning darkness;
I wait on time.

The stars cling to the night
 like bubbles in a glass of stale beer.
  A star does fall in a heartbeat.

The cat has seen it too;
 our conspiracy is complete.
We both smile,
 or at least the cat does;
it's hard for me to smile

when I am losing my secrets.

Timothy Swaim Johnson

OCTOBER 29

The sun's rays form dull rainbows

against the clouds.

There is a chill haze on the hills.

Into her cold blue mouth

the sky takes the sun.

Anne Yarosevich

LATE WINTER

The mist comes out of
  and goes into the snow
in between freezing and thawing,

jagged branches rake the sky
  pulling out its blue.
Leaves, grass and bark; brittle
parchment
  rustles like a gypsy's skirt
  in a late afternoon dance.

Balsam, hemlock husbanding their green
  against any depravity.
All life surrendering
  to the rude embrace of ice.

The snow is carnage
  waiting to be evacuated
on a stretcher of compassionate breezes.
  Warm breezes ignited by the wing-beat

of a single chickadee.

Timothy Swaim Johnson

JUNE ON WHITEFACE

Huddled close, dwarf foliage,

tea of labrador bursts its spume,

while along the jagged mountain ridge

miniature laurels bloom.

Bunchberry patches hug the ground

their dogwood blossoms green to white.

Lady slippers, white or pink gowned,

and trillium shelter 'neath hardwood's might.

Lofty mountain, rugged spine,

Faerie flowers garland this chine.

Anne Mausolff

SONG OF AUTUMN IN VERMONT

Frost lies down in patches
surrounding bushes and trees
beneath the freezing stars.
When morning breaks
the row of white pines on the lake
awaken to the crackling fires

of the blueberry bushes below them,
dark red flames lapping at
pagoda columned pines.
Even the lake itself
echoes: Fire! Fire!
Spring peepers softly trill

from hidden crannies.
An ancient toad, gaunt and warted, starts
belatedly to delve in the chilly earth.
A smoldering orange glow emerges
small at first, near the tops of mountains,
then runs riot over the wild valleys.

Bright yellow blasts of
leafy sunshine leap down
the cliffs of ridges
like mighty waterfalls.
On the granite top of the low
remote forest mountain

the pitch pines harbor lingering
birds, yellow vireos singing
back and forth mystical translations
from the final symphony of leaves.
Blue sky and sunlight
flood down

over the soft green pitch pine.
Tiny flying insects swarm aloft,
hovering over its branches,
catching the sunbeams,
glowing white like pale fairies,
dancing in the blue sky above the festive tree.

In the forests below
leaves tumble without ceasing:
beeches, maples, birches, oaks.
Dreary clouds roll in, darkening the earth.
Twilight rumbles,
smelling of mushrooms.

The golden mantle of the hills
grows bald, withered, threadbare.
Brown oak leaves swirl
in the clammy shivering wind.
Piercing November rains
pelt the earth unmercifully.

Rain pounds out its fury on the roof.
Gusts of wind rage
against our sanctuary.
Sheltered, for now, from the storm,
the two of us draw near
and whisper dreams of summer love.

Bruce Hesselbach

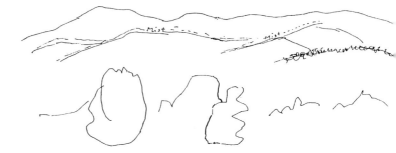

RESERVOIR

Mist hangs over the hills like smut.

The lake gathers ripples like grimaces.

Anne Yarosevich

ROCK TALK

Sand, hold my dreams
in the deeps of your grains.
In return I will make art
of your crystal prayers.

Anne Yarosevich

THE WATER'S EDGE

At the water's edge
  I see the universe
reflected in the sheen
  of the pond's surface
to the depths that
  any space probe
    can go.

Below the surface
  a newt undulates;
its exquisite silhouette
  flagging its life force,
breathing both air and water
  in complete adaptation
    of place.

A crisp crumpled leaf
  left over from Fall
sails upon the water's surface,
  delighting in being
its own spinnaker,
  bouncing from shore to shore
    at random.

The wind casts a handful
  of silver across the water
as wheat is sown on a field;
  the sky drinks up the glare,
the sparkle so dazzling
  the mind must rest
    a moment.

At the water's edge
  I see as much as need be seen,
my step as light as when
  looking in upon a sleeping child.
I need no voice
  at the water's edge
    at all.

Timothy Swaim Johnson

Old Pickles

SONG OF TWO OLD PICKLES
ON THE TRAIL

Sweet Gherkin

and Sour Dill

are far from being

over the hill.

Having hiked

two thousand miles

and more,

lived and worked

over three score,

they look forward still

to each new hill.

What a thrill

for sturdy

Sweet Gherkin

and Sour Dill.

Anne Mausolff

PFIZZLING OUT

Our romance was growing by the minute.
Bed was so much nicer when we were in it.
The cockles of our hearts were lovely and warm.
I should have known the signs of an approaching
storm.

Refrain: Pfizzling out
          We're just
          Pfizzling out

We usta be a hot ticket
Now our ticket's gone from red to blue
and our passion is just watered down glue.
And we, monsieur, are simply
                    pfizzling out.
                    Zout!

Anne Yarosevich

Caught in a time warp
a solitary hiker
joins the trilobites.

Anne Mausolff

BUDGET WOES

"We're over," he said.
"Please get out your budgets and
reflect on them."
SO.......
I got my budget out...
I reflected on it,
refracted on it,
I even genuflected on it!
And suddenly I could see myself.
It must have been the JOY of it!

Virginia Love

THIN ICE

Most people are not sure
  how thick ice should be
    before you can skate on it.

The experts say it should be
  two inches thick
    but how do you measure?

If I can get on the ice
  to drill a hole
    then I should be able to skate.

I did drill a hole
  in the edge of my pond once
    that showed the ice six inches thick.

The ice had looked thin to me
  but it was thick enough
    and I had a good skate.

Sometimes when I'm skating
  I imagine what it would be like
    to fall through.

I picture the ice cracking and rending.
  I careen and hurtle into the water,
    slabs of ice slide over my head and
      trap me; I drown.

I'm found floating face down
  in the Spring;
    the beavers have tugged on me.

My bills become past due,
  my lawyer is confused,
    my sister leaves messages
      on my answering machine.

The sink is full of dirty dishes.
There were poems I did not want read.
I'd always worn my seat belt.

I had not left instructions
on where I was to be buried
nor had I left a clever epitaph.
Amends and my bed go unmade,
someone else wins the lottery,
I didn't even have fifteen minutes.

The truth is I never listened
when they said I was skating on thin ice.

Timothy Swaim Johnson

POETRY CONFERENCE

I

One workshop leader has a bloody cough.

He reads a prologue till his hair falls off.

Like his college, he has a Mission Statement,

political agenda, tax abatement,

a loft in Soho, and a cottage on the Cape.

He talks of skulls; his poems defy a shape.

He thinks he's Handel or Eugene V. Debs.

His goatee and sandals look like Maynard Krebs

emoting angst in a peculiar whine.

The academics nod and say it's fine.

II

BROMA scanned the crowd, and shook her fist,

and said, "What happened to LARS LAGERKVIST?

Some say it was the women, some the booze;

some say the meatballs turned his brains to ooze!"

She swore an oath; her eyes were flaming swords.

The lesser poets trembled at her words.

III

Outside you can tell by the terrible stench

that there's some old geezer sitting on a bench

who says, "My neighbor's a very good fence;

through the evening snow I've tracked him hence

and now with the onset of rime and frost

I fear for my apples that I am lost.

Something there is that loves a map.

I think I lost mine near Toothless Gap."

Bruce Hesselbach

SOCKS

Having made the decision
  that this particular pair
of socks will not be laundered
  and worn again,
    I discard them.

As I take them off,
  I cast them off
into the waste basket.
  They've served their purpose
  and are worn out.

I remember when I bought them.
  They came in a pack of three;
basic brown cotton
  with reinforced heels and toes.

The many miles I walked in them
  slowly wore them down.
They knew my feet
  better than anyone,

and may even have developed
  a fondness for them.
I was fond of those socks
  and will miss them.

Timothy Swaim Johnson

ULTRA, ULTRA MODERN POETS

She said, "Just write a poem a day."

But do I really have that much to say?

Methinks thou thinks too much, old muse.

Too much thinking doth confuse.

Oh, these modern day writers of verse!

Their stream of consciousness a curse,

Without rhyme or reason they write and write,

Ambiguity in vogue, opaque as night.

Do readers understand the mess?

Are they too proud to confess?

There will always be those

Who know when the Emperor

is wearing no clothes.

Betty Hord Edelman

We were riding the rails,
a thirty six hour journey.
I to Eugene, she to find God
in whatever form He might appear.

My seatmate, Claire, sat in her
dowager's suit: English tweed,
Oxford shoes with laces
tied in neat double knotted bows,
 heavy, shiny stockings,
 the kind that make a swishing noise
when thickened thighs rub together in
mid-stride,
while her breasts cleaved unto themselves,
forming a single, sexless bust.

Then out came the margaritas and pretzels,
confounding first impressions.
Claire knew the ropes.
"Special price 'til five,"
"Let's go get another," she announced,
lumbering down the crowded aisle
toward the concession car.
She thought she was becoming
my best friend.

But how could I be best friends
with someone who had rudely
rejected the crumpled, worn, dollar bill
our waiter presented to her as change
after our dinner in the club car.
"It's a sign of Satan working against us,"
Claire announced, pointing to the faded paper,
forcing the beleaguered man to
shuffle through his wad
in search of an acceptable one,

43

one that hadn't been, as Claire said,
"Tarnished by Satan," a clean one
that respected the name of God
written on the bill.

As if that wasn't enough,
there was the list of complaints
about the dinner and service
she had carefully written
on the back of our bill,
"suggestions" Claire called them,
trying to soften the blow,
trying to make me agree with her.

Time for sleep, as my suspicions grew.
What signs from Claire's God,
what punishments from Satan might
be visited upon us?

And then it was dawn, first light.
As I awakened from fitful slumber
my bleary eyes focused on
the perfectly formed, unblemished red apple
Claire held out to me in her hand,
"Would you like some fruit?" she coaxed.

Then she was gone, detrained, and
in her place a card bearing
her hastily scribed parting words,
"Via Con Dios, my Darling!"

The crimson apple shimmered
in the rising sunlight.

Virginia Love

THE CAT'S BOOK OF HOURS

<u>Matins</u>
Chirrup, Chirrup.
As dawn stretches her pink toes
over the horizon
I rise from my plump pillow
I stretch out my left paw
        and bow,
I stretch out my right paw
        and bow
and say Good Morning to You.
        Purr, purr, purr ...r...r...r.

<u>Lauds</u>
Meow, meow.
Praise be to You Who has made my Universe.
Praise be to You for the tasty mice of the fields.
Praise be to You for the chipmunks in the stone wall.
Praise be to You for the squirrelettes in the maples.
Praise be to You for my three water dishes,
    in the house, by the front door, by the back door.
Praise be to You for the everflowing canister
    of chow bits; may it always be full.
Praise be to You for good smelling Special Diet.
Praise be to You for the tasty tidbits of chicken breast,
    ground turkey, NY strip sirloin.
Praise be to You for my clean litter box in the house,
    soft dirt and leaves under the trees.
Praise be to You for the hot sun in good weather,
    a warm stove in bad.
All praise and purr as long as my whiskers hold out,
    my claws stay sharp and strong.
Purr, purr.   Meow.

Prime
Meow.
Blessed be the hour when my food
        is fresh out of the can
          with odors that quiver my nostrils
          and textures that delight my tongue.
Blessed be this hour when I wash my cheeks,
        whiskers, eyebrows and chin.
Blessed be this hour of contemplation
          as I watch my mistress stretch in yoga.
Blessed be that I am still more supple than she.
Purr.

Terce
Chirrup.
I dance with the dancing leaves
 as they dance with the wind
        I leap and tumble on my own.
I pounce on a dry leaflet
        but the wind twirls it from my paw.
I listen to the pileated woodpecker chop his tree.
I hear the vole scud through the grass,
I smell the deer passing the oak.
I watch the bees buzz mint and marigold.
        All is alive with the joy of being.
        And so am I.
        Purr.

Sext
Chirrup.
Let the brook sing among the stones
Let the stones burble with the skaters
Let the skaters figure skate upon the water
Let the water hum a bass.
Let the fingerlings gape and dart
Let the bullfrogs croak and plunge
I lap the brook and jump from stone to stone.
        How great is the playground

You have provided for me.
Purr.

None
Chirrup.
How marvelous shines the sun through the trees.
Let the trees clap their leaves
        weave their roots
        shelter me
Protect me from a drizzle
        as I listen to the soprano droplets
        arpeggio around me
Let the ferns wave their fronds to the wind
        let me find shade beneath them at sun high.
Let the wide umbrella of the mullein
        be a haven in the storm
        How marvelous is the sunshine.
        How marvelous the rain.
        Purr.

Vespers
Twilight crouches in the west
Pats the sky with pink-toed, grey-furred feet.
The thrush throws a few tones
The downy drills a last dugout
I pad through my favorite hideouts
Then relax on my look-out
safe above the prowling dog
        the obtrusive coon
with my cat door a safety back-up.
        How beautiful the paws of twilight.
        Purr.

Compline
Cumulus clouds have hopped over the horizon.
But the Great Bear holds his sky
and Orion stands stalwart.
Praise and thanks to You
        for my every breath

49

my supple muscle
my living day.
Praise and thanks for Tom Cat Thunder
and Mama Cat Night.
I curl on my pillow
tuck my front paws in.
Thanks and praise for the best cat day ever.
Purr.

Anne Mausolff

SPARROWS

From homes beyond the Wall, the Mongols ride

through Northern China in the winter winds,

with camels bearing silver, salt, and hides,

to purchase sacred books and visit friends.

The way is hindered, as they near Peking,

by hordes of pilgrims coming from the west.

Despite the noise, they hear the sparrows sing

from cages where the sparrows are compressed.

"Buy captive sparrows," sellers loudly cry,

"And gather merit when you set them free."

And yet for every bird the Mongols buy,

the Chinese traders catch another three.

Light sparrows of the millet fields and weeds,

celestial lamas eating only seeds.

Bruce Hesselbach

PLEASE TOUCH

Light as a drop of morning dew

Her moist tongue dampens my cheek

Ebony eyes begging

Pat me, please touch,

Fawn colored tail thumping the floor

Body language questioning

"Will she pat me or will she holler

Pensey, go lie down ?"

I pat her silky golden ears

Press them gently

Scissors points folded together

          I run my hand over her back, softly stroking

She is all quivering motion, yet sitting as if

Taped to one spot

Wet kisses from her, caresses from me

She is satisfied. I can now say

          "Pensey go lie down

            On your rug, girl".

But when she needs attention

When her eyes signal "I need to be loved,

Please touch", the plea is understood.

II

Come Pensey come little girl

Here is your treat

I brought you a treat

From the restaurant

Hurry up, Pensey

Oh, it is so dark, so cold

Where are you little girl?

I can't see your fawn colored tail

Is it waving hello?

I can't see those shepherd ears

Rising above your thin collie face

Come Pensey, come welcome me home

Little girl it is dark and cold

And deathly quiet

Betty Hord Edelman

SAINT-SAENS' SWAN

A graceful bird undulates

through swelling waves

rippling tendons of cello, violin,

thrumming chords of golden harp --

a clipper, sails sheared,

and a broken heart.

Anne Mausolff

THE CAT

The cat waits by the door
for the thousandth time.

The door is opened,
she exits.

With a backwards glance
she suggests the door
be left open.

She won't be long
unless there is something
to detain her.

She sniffs the air
checking the temperature.

Her tail swiping,

she shoulders and hips
across the grass,

making tracks as old
as predation itself.

Timothy Swaim Johnson

FUR-BOMB

Fur-bomb lands on me

hot feet massage spine, shoulders,

to the tune of purr.

Anne Mausolff

CAPSIZED

The white moth
thrashes its one wing
treads water with needle toes.
It contorts its oval body
into a half moon.
Still its other sail
drags the surface
of the beaver pond
where the north wind
capsized it.
Gusts thrust and twirl it,
first into some sodden maple leaves
then onto a dry twig.
It clings there.
Suddenly, free of the water,
it quivers
sandwiched between
cold blasts and
warm rays.

Anne Mausolff

TELL TAIL

A sunburst skitters

across the snowy lea.

It trails a brush

as if to camouflage

its tale of blue prints.

Orange and crimson shimmer,

gold glints and sparkles

to halo the red fox

as it scampers in the sun.

Anne Mausolff

Transparent Walls

WESTON VILLAGE

Lovely village in the cushioning snow
How quiet, how clean the houses seem
The playhouse closed 'til Spring
The tiny library closed today
The postmaster gone to lunch
The fudge shop, a car out front
Behind the scene, work goes on
UPS picks up packages from the stores
Country store slices from the cheese wheel

Will be spinning across the U.S.A.
Furniture from the Bowl Mill

Will find homes thousands of miles away.
Behind frosted window panes
Townspeople talk of winter slowness
"Business will pick up," they say,
" when skiers come to Magic, Bromley, Stratton."

Lovely village nestled in the mountains
Lone cemetery at the edge of town
One church on Main Street, one on the hill
Services on Sunday, then folks gather
At the general store, visit awhile, sip coffee,
Enjoy a fresh baked muffin, take leave

Filled with the warmth of togetherness
Favorite newspaper tucked under arm.
Lovely village nestled in cushioning snow
Peaceful, serene this community life seems.

Betty Hord Edelman

OREGON ESCAPE

Battered little shacks

sit just enough back

from a stormy sea's reach.

Naked withered shacks

cringe on headland rack

scalped by seagulls' screech.

Abandoned dirty shacks

straggle on a tack

across the kelpy beach.

Anne Mausolff

NORMANDY

XIIIth Century village

XXth Century grass.

I stand there again

feeling the irony of anachronism.

All is well.

The stone farmhouse altered

by history, has slumped imperceptibly into its center.

Maybe the grass is XVIIth Century grass,

not XXth.

Had I lived forever, all I would know

is the bliss of the moment

which memory has shaped.

I can spend hours looking for pebbles,

proud of my unproductivity.

The sky is more than me, the stones, the grass.

I feel temporal, temporary, fading fast.

Anne Yarosevich

MARCH OF THE 10th

This godforsaken desert is a bitch.

We'd hoped for better pickings in the East,

for golden swag and slaves to make us rich,

and then become centurions at least.

Holding letters from my father's friend

to Trajan's camp I went at Antiochus,

meeting many farm boys at a feast,

young men of fortune ready to attend

the interview. We'll pay respects to Bacchus

and then become centurions at least.

Two wives I'll have in Africa and Britain

with triple pay and hoards of silver loot

and frequent leaves to speed my lengthy hitch.

The nubiles will appear, by Cupid smitten,

and military life's the fastest route

for golden swag and slaves to make us rich.

At Joseph's fortress where the fight began,

we soldiers soon had boiling oil to drink.

The hail of rocks and arrows never ceased

and several times the 10th broke rank and ran

for firebrands are hotter than you think.

We'd hoped for better pickings in the East.

Masada was the last stronghold to fall.

The heat was like an overhanging sword.

We died of thirst near by a poisoned ditch

and when at last our rampart reached the wall

the sight of corpses was our rich reward.

This godforsaken desert is a bitch.

                              Bruce Hesselbach

I LIKE THE CITY

There are people who hate the city --
I don't, I like the city, the energy, the motion
Crowds full of purpose hurrying
Along streets. I don't ask myself
To what purpose. Cars honking,
Drivers impatient to arrive somewhere else
In a hurry.

I like the coffee shops -- the smell
The city's favorite brand
Vermont's Green Mountain blend
Oregon's Starbucks and Java Man
I like them all. I like being
In a coffee bar brightly lit
People laughing, talking, planning,
Reading, writing, painting --
Perhaps another Hemingway,
Another Toulouse -Lautrec,
Sitting there at the corner table
Steaming mug in hand.
The city outside disappearing
In drenching rain.

I like the culture of the city
Libraries, Churches, Museums
Theaters, late night suppers,
I like the beautiful city
Lights like multi-colored stars
Shining in skyscraper windows.

Betty Hord Edelman

OVERHEARD IN PORTLAND

Hey Buddy, can you lend me a dime?

'Cause I'm bald like you,

But I'm a gangsta and

You're a hippie....ha,ha,ha

Hey Buddy, can you lend me a dime?

I been laughin' all night

not like the usual scene

Just seein' the way the world looks

through the bottom of my wine glass.

Hey Buddy......

Virginia Love

TO SHARE A STABLE

Beneath the bridge
Skeleton figures wrapped in rags
Huddle together seeking warmth
Over a tiny flame flickering in
The bottom of a rusty drum.
Sleet raps against the train window
I am warm and the pleasant smell
Of food fills the car. Christmas Eve,
4:30 P. M., night falling fast
Organ music playing " Away in the Manger"
Story of a homeless child
Finding shelter on a cold and distant night
In the little town of Bethlehem.
I watch the men moving around, changing places
Some lying on the ground, covered with newspapers --
All trying to keep warm in that landscape of
Iron and steel at the bottom of the world.
I wonder, is it random that they are there,
That I am here? I wonder if they can hear
The words to that ancient song.

Are they listening, remembering, wishing?
Wishing they could share the stable
Wishing they could sleep on beds of sweet hay
Wishing they could share love given the babe
Are they wishing they knew where the wise men
have gone?

                              Betty Hord Edelman

WINTER

On the train from Oradea

Cold, snowy, gray

Out the window a new scene,

Bleak, quiet, stark.

Virginia Love

THE PRISON

I'm living in a cell
something like a prison,
only the walls are transparent,
fluid, in motion.

They are the crowds in the streets,
     pushing, expressionless,
the children, dirty, ill, begging,
the cars that won't stop, the drivers
whose eyes won't meet mine,
the trucks and buses belching
thick, black clouds.
They are the stubborn bureaucrats, the
powerseekers who don't know
the rules have changed.

There is a road that leads
from this town,
but I can't find it.

Virginia Love

Neomi's Windowseat

NEOMI'S WINDOWSEAT

Sitting in a corner

with a bunch of plants

I am just another plant.

A funny looking one,

but passive tranquil

plant mentality nonetheless.

I have fair foliage

and my flowers are imaginary.

Anne Yarosevich

DOES IT MATTER IF MY DOG IS RIGHT OR LEFT PAWED?

Does it matter if
my dog is right or left pawed?
Who cares if Garth Brooks
ever sings another song?

Did Dione Lucas
ever eat pizza?
Will the sky ever run out
of its blue color?

I'm not haunted
by these questions.
I'm indifferent
to the answers.

You ask why
do I ask
the questions
if I don't care.

I answer
these are the only questions
left;
for me
all the others
have been answered.

Timothy Swaim Johnson

FEVER

Feet pounding rhythmically,

I run down a country road,

while beside me the

river rages and roars,

earth's blood, like mine --

  flowing, pulsing

as out of control as new love,

racing with the force of a sweeping wind

that could blow a door wide open,

leaving no secrets to be kept

and no turning back,

I run down a country road.

Virginia Love

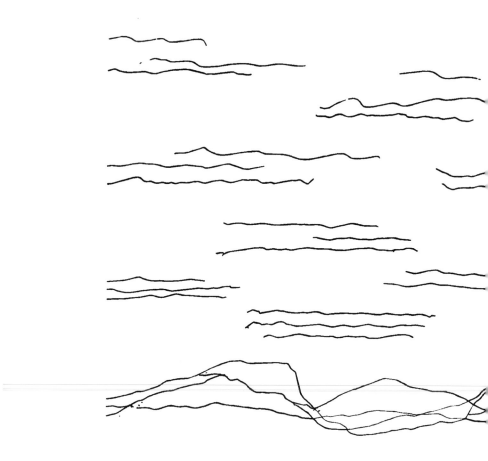

DAYBREAK

Grey light of dawn
pierced by birds
whose cries of joy are
bright as knives
wielded in love,
and yet not knives
but blazons of wholeness.
I want to pluck their voices
from the sky like fruit.
Rooms of birdsong
deafening, tangible.
This is of light,
this of sound.
Only their bright blue song
in this image of dawn
rescues me from
the niggardly fingers of fear
shortchanging my mind.

Anne Yarosevich

THE GARDEN

I forgot the clippers.
  Some of my best thinking
is done on the slow walk
  back to get them.

Gardening is the one activity
  that cannot be rushed.
Nature sets the pace
  which is that of a slow walk.

I can zip through the laundry,
  I can zip through shopping
but I cannot zip through gardening
  and do not want to.

With the retrieved clippers in hand
  I retrace my footsteps
reviewing plans
  and their reasonableness.

Things will get done,
  bridges will get built,
pages will get written
  but not before I have finished in the garden.

Timothy Swaim Johnson

REWIND - REPLAY

In the space of a shadow following
Bearing down, almost keeping step
Seventy years pass.
Now, rewind to replay.
There, the little desk in the dark corner
A child sitting, peacefully writing,
Learning the multiplication tables
Yellow pencil with its broad black lead
Smudges the coarse lined paper
Tiny fingers making numbers
To one hundred. Suddenly, she clutches
Her pencil tighter, the voices close,
Screaming epithets at one another.
Rage like bullets scoring targets.
In the crossfire, a child
Struggling to learn her numbers
$1 \times 1 = 1, 1 \times 2 = 2, 1 \times 3 = 3, 1 \times 4 = 4,$
Until the magic goal is reached, 100.
Was time enough remaining
To unlearn the powerful message
That other lesson's powerful drumbeat?
A hundred years, reached by few
In fast forward.

Betty Hord Edelman

WALKING AWAY FROM THE SINK

Walking away from the sink
  I wipe my hands
    on the seat of my jeans.

The day is past
  its point of no return;
    so is the season.

I step over a threshold;
  the list of things I've done
    is longer than the list
      I want to do.

The wait for the tomatoes
  to ripen is over.
    It was a good year
      for the elderberries.

Pumpkins tastefully arranged
  at the door step.
    A small cache of wormless apples
      that may or may not keep.

The new wing feathers
  of the Toulouse geese,
    ready for the Fall flight
      they'll never take.

The rooster crowing
  that his job is done for the Summer.

Abandoned tent caterpillar nests
  strewn about in trees
    matching my disregarded
      thoughts.

This is the last Summer
  the dog will jump
    in and out of the jeep
      with ease.

Perhaps I stayed off
  the receding tide of my hairline
    another year;
      I don't care anymore.

The catalog orders
  arrive daily:
    one hundred Narcissi Actaea bulbs,
    Beans's boots size 9 1/2 M.

The journey continues.
  I plod with the seasons,
    accepting disappointments,
      renewing promises.

Timothy Swaim Johnson

THE TARN

The water like thick cold sapphire
we walk to it
across a field of frozen grass
so crunchy it is almost edible

Have you ever felt
the presence just behind the sky
just like we were all
holding our breath
in some part of us
we rarely recognize

We make the ocean flow
we people it
with our utmost desires

Anne Yarosevich

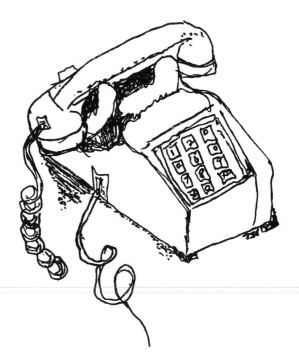

CONVERSATIONS WITH GOD

At first it comes as a whisper
  because one has not learned to listen.
Concentration is necessary.

One cannot hear anyone
  even God
if one is not listening.

One way to learn how to listen
  is to buy a self-help book
where someone else makes money
  telling one how to help oneself.

"Listen my children and you
  Shall hear
Of the midnight ride of
  Paul Revere."

Pale horse, pale rider.

It's all in how you listen up
  "Be still and know that I am God."
We never did too much talking anyway,
  God only knows.

I'm getting older;
  have more time to talk
and listen.

Did I miss something
  that was said?
Can you repeat that now
  I'm ready to listen?

I'm too far gone to change
  but it might be fun
if we discussed a few things.

Like why is the art
  of conversation dying?
And did I help kill it?
  God only knows!

"Sorry I'm not in right now,
  please leave a message at the tone."

Is this my real life
  or is this a test?
Had this been a real life
  would you have left instructions?

When there were emergencies
  my local radio station was not
much help.

Except for the music
  which I did listen to
waiting for You
  to get in touch with me.

                    Timothy Swaim Johnson

CONSTANCY

Somewhere, Philomela is singing
Her sad lament.
Orpheus is playing his lyre
Blending order, pain, constancy.
The ashes of my beloved
Lie enclosed in brown box
On the polished oak.
The deer, hundreds, starving
On frozen midwestern plains
Cruel winter of death!
Somewhere, out there
Philomela is singing
Her sad lament
Orpheus is playing his lyre
Blending order, pain, constancy.

Artemis, silver queen of night
Lights the waves, pointing the way
For lost Odysseus -- guiding him home
Over the blue Mediterranean.
Night queen guiding fishermen home
Across the Sea of Galilee
Centuries gone by.

Tonight, I watch her light
Shining on the Sea of Cortez
Guiding wanderers over the waves
Centuries gone, centuries to come
Artemis shining in the night
Golden Apollo in the day
Philomela singing her sad lament
Orpheus playing his lyre
Blending order, pain, constancy.

Betty Hord Edelman

HOURS IN THE DAY

I count the hours,
occasionally miscounting.

Sometimes there are too many.
Sometimes there are not enough.

I've lost more hours
than I care to admit.

My mind an hourglass,
with the sand stuck.

Jog my memory
and thoughts flow.

Rack my brain
for a grain of thought.

No future,
no past,
only the Holy Instant,

which is timeless;
without seconds nor minutes,
never to be ours.

Timothy Swaim Johnson

MEMORY LANE

I've twelve-stepped most
  all of my addictions:
rather gracefully for the most part.

My crippled and insane life
  is noticably more serene now
with the help of my higher power.

I've made peace with the past
  and have become fond of recall.
I like to look back on the good times.

I walk down memory lane
  searching for happier times:
this is nostalgia...
  the last of my addictions.

Timothy Swaim Johnson

AWAKENING

Early morning - March
I awaken to wind howling,
or is it wolves?

Just before first light
sly shiftings of light and shadow
can beguile or frighten.

Faint rooftop scratchings
become probing paws,
 claws of vengeful intruders
unraveling the veil of sleep.

A restless awakening,
this kaleidoscopic view of space and time,
this almost spring morning.

Then gradually light
defines familiar objects and
it is the budded branches of the crab apple tree
swaying, knocking on my window,
that finally break the spell.

Virginia Love

A Closer Look

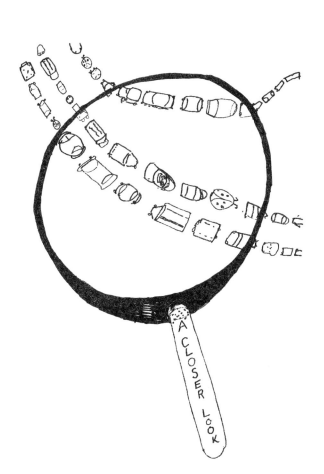

FIRST LIGHT

It is early morning now,

just after first light.

Outside, a light frost glistens,

and there is just one strong star

 rising in the eastern sky.

Through the branches I see it,

steadily climbing, limb upon limb,

and I think, if only I can hold this

 in my view as a point of light,

then I just might be able to abide truth,

to gather the strength to place my foot

 on the floor and rise,

to bear the weight of loss,

to begin another day.

Virginia Love

AT FIRST GLANCE

He walks the walk of pride, leading his own parade,
With a mismatched pair of oxen, plodding,
   hauling their odorous load.
The pace is slow and yet he knows
There is somewhere else to go.

With a mismatched pair of oxen, plodding,
He walks the walk of pride.
The pace is slow and yet he knows
There is somewhere else to go.

He walks the walk of pride, but a closer look reveals,
  feet that shuffle instead of stride, and eyes
   that don't really see,
He walks the walk of pride, but a closer look reveals
His hand holding fast to a walking stick,
  a wry smile on his lips.

Feet that shuffle instead of stride, and eyes
  that don't really see.
The pace is slow and yet he knows
There is somewhere to go
His hand holding fast to a walking stick,
  a wry smile on his lips
There is somewhere yet to go, he knows,
There is somewhere to go.

Virginia Love

Light brown hair cascading to her shoulders
Sunlit, how it shines
Above the dark brown eyes
Sparkling with youth's
Love of challenge, love of change.
She is sitting in the white, hot sand
Getting her hair braided
Her scalp pulled tight to her head
Twist, pull, twist pull to shape
Pins moist in saliva to hold
My head hurts to watch
The patient Mexican woman
Skilled at her business.
My granddaughter's hair
Is wavy, long and bouncy.
The new design is taking a long time.
The stylist calls her assistant
A crowd gathers
Rhea likes the attention.
Her hair hangs in strips
Like chili peppers drying
Why am I thinking " Medusa "¿
The end is near, her crown covered
In rows looking newly ploughed
My granddaughter is beaming
She loves the way it looks
    She is thirteen.

                Betty Hord Edelman

MADSONG AND HEADACHE

Strange that I should think of her

when my head's been throbbing all day

and all the world's to me like one

colossal hangover.

But there's pain enough in the world to drive

a body mad,

and her madness was pain

for 26 years, longer than anyone

should ever endure.

When I see the madwomen of the City

repeating their phrases again and again

I think of people in pain

and how it freezes their thoughts

in agony again and again in the same old round:

why oh why oh why

dear god

oh why oh why oh why?

But I don't have bitter thoughts (of anyone but myself)

and we didn't have J. Edgar Hoover persecuting us

and we didn't live as Communist pariahs raging against

the bland conservative smug society of 1955.

No, she had every reason to be grateful and happy,

every reason except

except

    a childhood in the depression

    dirt poor

    her father dead when she was but 12

    and the doctor telling her brother, "Now you're

the man of the family" when he was 14

    and he had a paper route

    and someone stole his bike

101

and her mother got by as best she could

    she was a strong woman

    but my mother was not.

By 1955 she had everything to live for and all the
blessings of life:

    a place in the suburbs with roses

    like Ozzie and Harriet or the Life of Riley

    a devoted husband

    a boy who loved her

and a newborn baby

        except

that baby wasn't a girl as she had hoped

and life with two children is hard

and the money got tight

and she got depressed and just couldn't handle it

    and her sanity fell apart.

Pilgrim State

in 1955

grotesque brick prison and torture chamber

to shock you back to reality

or shock you into permanent decline.

Chains in the attic

Russians dripping cold water

on Nicolai Gogol's head

The ancient Kelts would take a mad person

and ride with them on horseback

at a breakneck speed.

Or sometimes they would tie a rope around the

madman's waist, and tow him behind

a ten-oared boat,

as fast

as the rowers

could row.

God help us if he didn't die

life is fragile

the heart is fragile

No, I wasn't 12 as Ginsberg was;

it started when I was only 5,

but I remember the agonies

the delusions to ease the pain.

Her long lost brother was next door:

why wouldn't they let her see him!

Her husband at work would come home to her!

Why wouldn't he hurry home?

There would be money and food

"abundance" of everything.

104

She wouldn't have to deal with it again,

she wouldn't have to stand it!

All the world formed a league against her

to foil these utopian delusions.

All the world

but not we children.

She never stopped believing in us.

Though we cringed behind the doors when she raved

and fretted ourselves how to save her.

When push came to shove, we were just selfish

little brats

unable, unwilling to help

no better disciplined than she was

too frightened to try to understand

angry at times

even contemptuous, mocking.

Why couldn't she wake up?

Wake up! Get rid of these delusions!

No, she could never completely renounce them

gnashing her teeth, crying and shouting for help

Who in the 50s had help for the lunatic?

No, they had nothing but electric shocks

wards like a concentration camp

dehumanizing condescension

and the religious crazies

spoonfeeding their own delusions to the helpless and
weak

but at least they had a kind word or two

a little encouragement

There was damn little of that for a hopeless disease

progressive

coarsening

degrading

leaving the afflicted with no dignity

just cigarette after godawful cigarette, eight of them

going in the house at the same time

and ashes in the food

and the stove burners left on

     wandering around with a flatfooted gait

     puffing away, lost in some unearthly void

     sleepless, worried, unable to rest

      guzzling bituminous tea

      and reading incomprehensible books

pouring over the pages that made no sense

as if by some magic incantation to calm

her wild delusions.

Mommy! Mommy! Mommy!

In all your misery you were a good mother to me

and I love you with all my heart.

I hate that disease and what it did to you

      your last years were bitter ones

      a wreck of your former self

though not without humor

not without bravery

and love.

We gave you that daughter you missed

      but goddamn it

you hardly lived to see her

your poor little chest heaving in and out

trying to breath with emphysema

      up all night at my brother's

when Dad was in the hospital

      up all night and wandering back and forth

they didn't know how to calm you

no doctor to minister to a mind diseased

and those awful cigarettes

and your final bout with lung cancer

108

and the two grandchildren at your funeral

and the red roses on your coffin

Oh Come oh Come Emmanuel

the minister intoned

And ransom captive Israel

That mourns in lonely exile here

And the long lost brother saying

She suffered too much

His was a loss,

one who always looked up to him

worshipped him

Some brotherly kindness he did her

in her childhood days

cancelling out his unbroken succession of failures

109

making him always a star in her eyes

Yes his was a loss,

but greater the loss of the children

for the love of a mother and a son

is something magical and wonderful.

I see it in my own son today

and I feel it in my heart now

though twelve years have passed

and I ask

WHY DID THIS HAPPEN¿

this inexorable unmerciful plague

this piercing unbearable pain of the mind

this madness of unremitting agony¿¿¿

No one can say why.

There is no one to take the blame.

It's part of life

110

it's part of me

and I'll remember

           and her insanity will be

my insanity

           and her pain will be

my pain

           forever and a day

forever and a day.

Bruce Hesselbach

111

Car trouble at the Plaza

CAR TROUBLE AT THE PLAZA

Once in awhile your truck or car
just won't start.
Then it is time to try
to fix it yourself.
The owner of this truck
is doing just that.
He got it to start
but then it stalled flat.
He did that again
and again.
Then he sat in his truck
and talked to a friend.
He forgot about the truck.

Anne Yarosevich

GINGER ON THE VIOLIN

She collects harmonies
  in her soul.
Chords reside in her heart.
  Musical notes line up
    in her mind.

She brings out songs
  on occasion,
one after another
  released at bow
    and string point.

She is a sounding board.
  Life's music
is her music
  as closely felt as a silk chemise,
as sublime as
  Van Gogh's colors,
as spirited as
  a mountain echo.

Timothy Swaim Johnson

PRETZEL BOY

She slammed the fresh dough down

    slapped it here, there,

    kneaded it to her will.

When it pot-bellied out

    she punched it, hard,

    straight to the solar plexus.

She twisted it into a figure-eight, tight,

    and when it slipped its hitch

    whiplashed it into place

    and sprinkled salt on the wound.

    When he was seventeen

        he broke the knot, the hard crust.

        In a paroxym of revenge

        he punched, twisted, stabbed

        not her, the massive matron,

        but the malleable neighbor girl.

        Anne Mausolff

114

EMILY

She marveled at falling snow
Muted sound, trees in ermine
Matching ground
She marveled at the village church
Blending in -- in white
Slender steeple stretching high
Searching for that magic light
She marveled, in her words:

> *To see the Summer Sky*
> *Is Poetry, though never in a book it lie --*
> *True Poems flee --* . . .

She marveled at the village life
Neighbors, friends, and kin
Faithful and faithless, troubled and serene
Roots planted deep
Generation to generation
Secure in final sleep -- In:

> *A house that seemed*
> *A swelling of the ground....*

She marveled at it all
Discarding what could not fit
Such intellect, wisdom, wit:

> *The soul selects her own society*
> *Then shuts the door....*

Lines penned a century ago
Like the unmatched purity of snow
Fill me with an inward glow.
I marvel to find the key
Unlock the door to select society.

Betty Hord Edelman

VALEDICTION

Once a little pixy, full of fun,
took me by the hand to wander on
around our block, the several sights to see:
a squirrel, a flower, the sound of far-off trains,
a caterpillar's leaf, a bee.
The world was our discovery.
Now we're long gone from those domains
yet some dim trace of them remains.

Pictures I have, and movies of her, too.
Projects she made with cardboard, paste and glue.
She had an operation on her eyes
when only three. Such fear we felt! Such pains!
To see our daughter brave the knife
when she meant more to us than life.
Her sight returns; the panic wanes
yet some dim trace of it remains.

Through many bold adventures and some tears
we travel down that trail of childhood years
and find her presently in senior high
looking in at college windowpanes.
The time has finally come, but I
can't find the way to say goodbye.
How harsh to leave! So time ordains
yet some dim trace of her remains.

                    Bruce Hesselbach

JULY 17

I have come here to thank you

for nothing specific

just everything that has touched me

in all the different ways

your Being has of making my life

my life

and my perception

unique.

Let the last fly buzzing me

take my message to you.

Thank you.

I may never understand,

but in this moment

I thank you in love.

Anne Yarosevich

Feel the Rhythm

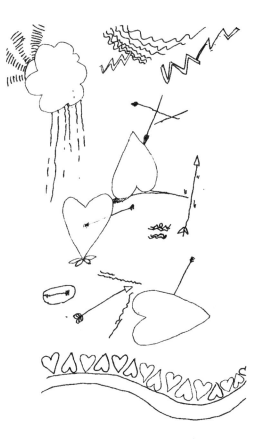

FEEL THE RHYTHM

The first time
  I danced to Lester Lanin's
    Orchestra

I was wearing a tuxedo
  and had just had
    a nice dinner.

I was young, handsome,
  a good dancer
    and ready.

With a debutante in my arms,
  a beat in my heart,
    I danced.

First a fox trot,
  then a two step,
    then a tango.

"They asked me how I knew
  My true love was true,"
    Dip, turn, swing.

My smile was easy,
  my style in fashion;
    the world was my oyster.

Other dancers gave us room.
  round and round we went.
    The orchestra played on.

To this day I still feel the rhythm.

Timothy Swaim Johnson

121

EROS

Alone in the woods
I play to your presence
which watches my passing with love,
that I may take comfort
in my delight of rocks and mosses,
and stones marked with symbols --
the messages and stories
of geologic love.

You follow me to a clearing
where the trees pull back
like spectators in a parade.
I lie down so that the sun
can envelop my body
in a bliss that makes me smile.
You are somewhere in the pines
that front the clearing,
rousing the birds, who call now.
And yet you are in my mind
meeting its wild call,
opening me to never,
saying goodbye to a cloud
called memory
sliding up the sky.

Anne Yarosevich

HEARTS -- TRUMPS?

As she stilted across the parking lot
her fuzzed hair puffed out
on each lobe
in a yellow heart-shaped hair-do
that perched
atop a rouged heart-face.
Pierced by staring, blue-shadowed eyes,
the wide forehead
that tapered to the chin,
sat above a chute
that plunged like a waterfall
into her bosom-pool.
The heart-scalloped neck
of her open blouse
formed a foamy frame
that cascaded
into a chasm.
On each side, the black walls
of her narrow leather coat
sheared away from shoulder to ankle.
Thus she tripped on feet squeezed
into heart-pointed loafers.
Many-hearted lady --
a heart seine
to trap unwary fish
in any kind of tide.

Anne Mausolff

GARDEN OF BEULAH

To be quite brief, and shun excess,

my name is Carol, my realm Niceness.

In the Garden of Beulah, where plums abound,

in the Zone of the Ocean, with the sound

of balmy currents and delights,

whereby we listen through the nights

to twanging of the guitar'd moon,

the lyre, the mariner's bassoon,

the harp whereon the Sirens play

in wistful notes their dreamy lay,

on friendly sand we have a tryst,

enfolded in the Ocean mist.

Bruce Hesselbach

PRIMAL STIRRINGS

Sweet memory of first sex:
making out with a boy
against the curve of a grand piano,
driven by a new and different feeling
This must be pleasure, I thought.
His hands chafed my breasts
through my shetland sweater.
The room was geting hotter.
He wants something, I thought.
"Stop," I croaked.
He looked at me with a wry grin.
"Bitch," he said.
And walked away.

Anne Yarosevich

FIRST FIRE

In the light of morning's first fire
as waking coals sound their crackling chatter,
your words charge the air
with life and laughter, branding
the early morning stillness.

Now ablaze, the fire warms.
You stand steady,
deliberate, affirming,
planning the graphics of your day
in dimension, color, and space.

Hat in hand,
"I'm out of here," you say,
"a guy's got to work."
And away you go
to share your energy with the world,
each moment an enchantment,
your dance with life.

I damp the fire down,
leaving diminished flames to
smolder and mellow,
like the downy robe of love.

Virginia Love

Tower of Babble

IL TROVATORE

Il trovatore
canta il su'amore
alla ballerina
che si chiama La Tina:
  "O mi amore
    nella casa al torre
    sotto il tu' occhio
    sgardame al ginocchio.

    Il tu' amore
    nel mio cuore

    molto ma molto
    da tanto in tanto
    presta tu' orrecchio
    al mio canto."

The troubadour
sings of his love
to the ballerina
known as La Tina:
  "Oh, my love,
    in the house by the tower,
    beneath your eye
    see me on my knee.
  Your love
    in my heart
    ever so much
    ever and anon
        bend your ear
        to my song."

Anne Mausolff

VILLE-VILLAGE

Le soleil touche
les batîments
avec un main tendre
du matin.
Traversant la rue des Batignolles
je vois apparaître
les os ivoires des residences
et je sens l'odeur libérant
du café.
Dans la chaleur d'une autobus
j'amène mes brosses, peintures et papier
vers la Seine
ou coulent certainement nos amours.
Aujourd'hui je vais peindre les pierres
des quais
car chacune a son caractère
et son histoire.
Pierres grisâtres, avec souvent
les petits blémis du temps. . .
Malgré le soleil qui chante
maintenant
en traversant les toits.

The sun touches
the buildings
with the tender hand
of morning.
Crossing the rue des Batignolles
I see appearing
the ivory bones of residences
and I smell the freeing aroma
of coffee.
In the warmth of an autobus
I am taking my brushes, paints and paper

to the Seine
where surely our loves still flow.
Today I shall paint the stones
of the quays
because each one has a character
and a history.
Grey old stones, often marked
with the little blemishes of time,
despite the sun which sings
now
as it crosses the rooftops.

Anne Yarosevich

THE BELLE JAR SANS MERCI

Aujourd'hui je suis perdu
Parce que je suis dérangé,
Je suis rien de tout.

Le mal de coeur
Me suit toute la journée
Et ne s'arrête pas.

Avec une cloche sur ma tête
Je marche seul au brouillard.
Je suis désolé.

Today I am lost
Because I am deranged,
I am nothing at all.

My heartache
Follows me all day long
And does not stop.

With a hat on my head
I walk in the fog alone,
I am desolate.

Timothy Swaim Johnson

FEET

J'aime caresser tes pieds
car ils sont nerveux et timides
comme des adolescents trops grands
pour leur vêtements d'enfance.
Tes pieds, légèrement endurcis,
réflètent le passé et ton caractère:
grand, sensible, attirant.

I like to caress your feet
because they are jumpy and shy
like adolescents too tall
for their childhood clothes.
Your feet, slightly calloused,
reflect the past and your nature:
large, sensitive, attractive.

Anne Yarosevich

AMANECER

Abro los ojos al amanecer
El sol persigue la noche
Triunfante, el sol salta
del lejano paisaje
Estoy viva -- otro dia ha comenzado

I open my eyes to the dawn
The sun is chasing the night
Triumphant, it leaps out
From behind the distant landscape
I am alive -- another day has begun

Betty Hord Edelman

VENIȚI CU MINE

Veniți cu mine
mergem pe jos la munte
aici si acolo

O să vedem floarile si pasări
O să auzit ecoul trecutului
peste tot
cintec foarte fromos

Come with me
Let's go to the mountains,
Here and there

We will see flowers and birds,
We will hear echoes of the past,
Everywhere
A beautiful song.

Virginia Love

Enigmas

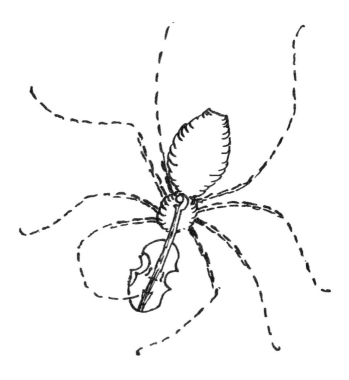

THE BROWN RECLUSE

She dances a dance.

She plays a hidden game.

Cunningly she hides herself and her

intentions

for she need not spin nor weave a web.

Her violin wreaks havoc as she plays her

striking tune.

Too late, intruder, do you step back.

More insidiously than de Medici has she

killed you.

The Brown Recluse.

Anne Mausolff

PUZZLE

Lying flat, pressed tightly there

No stirring of leaves or air

They cannot hear, touch or see

They could speak if they were free

How is it possible the years did fly

And I not heed the abandoned's cry

What kind of mother am I

Full term birth to them deny?

Betty Hord Edelman

GRAVITY

I'm grateful I was not present
  at the happening of
    the Big Bang.

For sure I would have been
  scorched and
    blown to bits.

The din would have been
  devastating. Probably,
    I would not have survived.

I never took implosion well;
  expanding neutrons notwithstanding
    vertigo is one of my dreads.

I never want to get
  any closer to the Big Dipper
    than I am.

For all I know the Sun
  could end up rising
    in the West.

Which would make me completely late
  for the occupations I have
    that take eternity.

It's not over yet;
  I'm still catapulting.

Here I am floating through
the universe with the earth
attached to my feet.

Forever trying to get my bearings,
chasing Aurora, bores and Alice.

Catching falling stars
and putting them in my pocket
gratuitously gravity free.

Timothy Swaim Johnson

THE SHADOWS

The trees,
the snow,
the shadows
  long blue shadows
    prostrate and strewn.

Shadows paying homage
  to the trees
    to which they are bound.

Shadows,
  the tangible part of nature's soul,

migrate across the Winter scape
bearing witness to the Sun's
    Glory.

Measuring my thoughts
  in increments.
    Fade in fade out,
silhouetted by the wings of hawks and angels.

                    Timothy Swaim Johnson

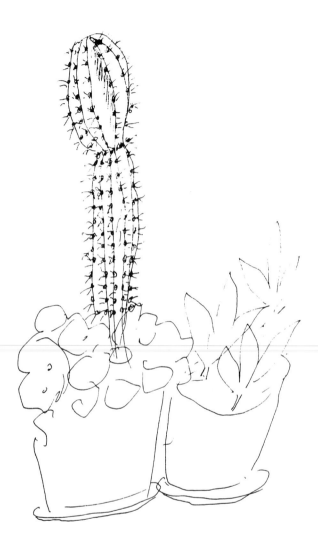

MAYBE

The cactus without spines

is defenseless

The world without pain

is defenseless.

Anne Yarosevich

ON THE CHANCE I TOOK HAVING MY PORTRAIT PAINTED BY SOMEONE I HARDLY KNEW

Searching for essence
Undefined,
Is it me?
Or is it thee?

Virginia Love

GRASS

Greenly

the grass toucheth

my feet with its shade

In the soft deeps of it

is solace for millions of feet.

Anne Yarosevich

TRAPPED INSECT

The barlabat beats against the windshield.

Out there is light;

Out there is field

And sky in which to romp and sing.

The barlabat beats up and down the side.

Gateway to port

He does not sense

As he titter-tatter-toes upon the glass.

The barlabat beats along the shield,

Skitter-legged

Scatter-brained

Wasting his life for a change of direction.

Anne Mausolff

THE RESONANT DOCTOR

"Anglia Dulandi lacrymis moveatur"

Join in the echoing Renaissance feast

Of difficult courses without surcease.

How many fantasias withal?

Not less than six, seven or nine.

Down in the vales of the bridge and damp

Ox, first arises the clear flowing spring,

Weeping into a never failing stream,

Lady Leighton's moonlit dancing dream,

A wedding between the Viol and the Harp.

No protesting hand invents these

Decorated repeats, this airy farewell.

Bruce Hesselbach

149

MY FUNERAL

How to prepare for my funeral;
  get my life in order,
race to the end
  at the speed of dark.

When they celebrate my passing
  I will not be a witness.
but I will be there
  as though taking a nap.

Hopefully, the undertaker
  tucks away my second chin.
He can leave in the gray;
  I always thought it was distinguished.

In my best Brooks Brother suit
  with a favorite tie.
My boarding school cuff links.
  My collapsed veins drained
    of unrealized dreams.

My underwear clean,
my socks matching,
my wingtips pointing up.

A little eye-liner,
some Touch 'N Glow
to cover the pallor.

Flowers, organ music,
  light through stained glass.

Kleenex, hard benches,
  permission for time off

for the mourners;
me the only one not on schedule.

Liszt, Schonberg and Bach will be played,
The Prophet, Rilke and Merton will be read.
The 23rd Psalm will bring forth a tear or two.

Testimonials to my wit
    and sagacity will be offered.
They might even touch on
    my non-existent charity
    and forward thinking.

For one grand hour I'll be missed;
    a nice funeral;
        too bad I will not be there.

Timothy Swaim Johnson

SILENT SENTINELS

Wreaths of Roses

Carnations and Lilies

Silent Sentinels

Surround the pine box --

Gray-lined

Funeral fragrance permeates

Close space

Covers death

Betty Hord Edelman

SESTINA FOR MUHAMED ISA

Dedicated to Mt. Kailasa, also known
as Kang Rinpoche, the holy mountain.

Ladaki by birth, by choice a traveler
who in his lifetime many lands would pass,
Muhamed Isa was unique. The wind
of fortune brought him wealth and fame. A rock
of faithfulness, enduring bitter cold
and hunger, making heavy burdens light,

he guided many expeditions. Light
jokes were not his style; a traveler
through Tibet must be on guard. The cold
is deadly; wolves and ravens watch each pass.
When one seeks pasture, all he sees is rock.
When one craves water, all he finds is wind.

Chang Tang -- the homeland of the icy wind
where salty lakes deep blue in wintry light
are girt about by endless sky and rock.
No fertile meadows for the traveler,
but flows of ice and fields of snow. The pass
at Nimalung replaces air with cold.

And then you see them, in uncanny cold,
the Himalayas, soaring over wind,
each cloud-surpassing summit, time-carved pass
as huge as Earth, yet flying high and light
where air can barely reach, and traveler
must plant each foot as slowly as a rock.

A stroke at Sakadzong caused him to rock
and tumble down half paralyzed and cold,
and nothing could be done. The traveler
gave up the ghost. A sighing mountain wind
sang dirges on his grave. In daybreak's light
the caravan moved on to Tugri Pass.

In time the grave drew notice. It came to pass
that shrieks and groans were heard from under rock
and dreadful apparitions' eerie light
affrighted villagers who felt the cold
unquiet stones and heard a moaning wind:
dire portents from a restless traveler.

How shall the traveler ascend the pass?
What wind will bear him from this frozen rock
to Kailasa's cold and holy light?

Bruce Hesselbach

MARBLEHEAD, 1953

Straight-backed, my grandmother sat.
"He was a wonderful man," she said.
Who was she talking to?
I, the child, hardly knew.

I had only seen the ambulance,
its blood red lights flashing.
The stretcher bearing the ashen mound
seemed to float down the stairs
as they carried him past.

And then there were the clusters of whispers,
the large staring eyes, the weeping,
As the black hole of grief caved in on itself.

So this was death, the not coming home.
A silence not to be touched.

Virginia Love

ONCOLOGIST

A perfect day when all earth is singing.

A rare moment of peaceful content.

I am happy to be exactly where I am --

here, with you standing beside me

gazing out , over the sun-jeweled

Sea of Cortez. Your keen brown eyes

watching gulls and pelicans feasting

in the water. Suddenly,

in a dark and somber mood you say,

" I think I would like to come back a pelican;

look at that bird's grace, his beauty."

The dreadful cold winter returns

as chills of sadness ripple my spine.

Why is he thinking about the future,

unknown, terrifying?

I look at his handsome young face.

His strong body in its prime.

Vision of a little boy

in a red stocking cap,

chin strap tied to protect

him from the cold.

Protect him from all the cold

in a capricious world.

"Something is missing in your words," I say,

" What else do you admire about the pelican?"

" His freedom. "

Robe of contentment lost.

This wonderful present dissolved in thought.

Your life -- the endless struggle, the daily

battle against a foe, relentless, malignant.

Melancholy lifts as we watch the pelican

white wings casting a shadow in the sand

as he soars higher and higher

in silence, alone, free.

Betty Hord Edelman

SMART BOMB

Hail to thee, Smart Bomb,

brainless as ever thou art.

Disinterested as any shogun

unfeeling, ill begun,

you glide astray your mark

snuffing out hospitals for your lark,

homes, schools, bridges. What fun

to dismember babes, mothers, sons.

Oh bomb so great and smart

Oh steel without a heart.

Anne Mausolff

THE LAST APPLE

The burnt umber laciness
　of late Autumn grass
speckled with sienna
　leaves embedded,

crackle sweetly with each step;
　answering whispers from a birch
mixing the balsam scent
　wafted by sun waves,

reflected in the sheen
　of silver flecked water.
The breeze caressing
　with rustling sighs,

making even fainter
　the call of departing
　　geese.

My teeth snap the skin
　of the last apple I have picked;
the sweet causes pain
　in my jaw under my ears

as saliva rushes
　to mix with
　　apple juice.

With each bite I will store
　essence, to last
through the Winter,
　to flow again in Spring.

Timothy Swaim Johnson

NOTES ON THE POETS

BETTY HORD EDELMAN has an MA in English from
Fairleigh Dickinson University. At Fairleigh she studied
poetry with Adonis Decavalles, and later spent a summer
in Wroxton, England, where she continued her studies,
focusing on British poetry. A retired high school teacher,
Betty lives with her husband in Andover, Vermont, near
beautiful Markham Mountain. They have two sons and
four grandchildren. As Editor of *The Spark*, the Vermont
newsletter of the United Nations Association, Betty
keeps abreast of important global issues. Her favorite
activities are walking and reading.

BRUCE HESSELBACH grew up on Long Island. A graduate of Yale (BA 1972) and Villanova (JD 1975), he worked for a Manhattan law firm before moving to Vermont in 1989. In 1996, he started his own law firm in Brattleboro, Vermont. His poems have been published in *Waterways, The Lyric, The Piedmont Literary Review, Reflect, Spellbound,* and *Poetic Justice.* He has also contributed humorous articles to *Lawyers Weekly USA* and *Word.* He has climbed over 200 mountains in the Northeast and nearly all of Vermont's Long Trail. He lives in Newfane with his wife Carol and children Erica and Brian.

TIMOTHY SWAIM JOHNSON wrote his first serious poem in 1996. After taking the plunge, it is a rare week that goes by without his writing a poem. For him, poetry is the fourth dimension of the soul and spirit. He lives and thrives off grid (with no public utilities), on a dirt road, off a dirt road, in Chester, Vermont, homesteading with the animals and garden he writes about in his poems.

VIRGINIA LOVE is a co-founder of the Londonderry Poets. Her poetry is inspired by the desire to communicate the essence of an emotion or an experience. She is also a perceptive observer of nature, a central theme in her life and work. Her interests include running, hiking, and traveling. Her more recent travel adventures included a year abroad living and teaching in Romania. She also studies the violin, and plays with the Main Street Arts String Band and the Southern Vermont Youth Orchestra. She is the mother of three sons and currently lives in the village of Chester, Vermont.

ANNE MAUSOLFF, after years in classrooms and
libraries, abandoned academia to run her own Cross
Country ski business in Vermont. Always an avid
backpacker and telemark skier, she spends much time in
the outdoors.   One of the amazing things about Anne is
that she has hiked the entire length of the Appalachian
Trail not once, but twice. She will soon complete
ascents of all of the Northeast's 111 highest mountains.
She lives in a charming country home which she built
herself. Her extensive world travels include a recent
expedition kayaking in Alaska. The great outdoors
inspires much of her poetry as well as her watercolor
painting and calligraphy.

ANNE YAROSEVICH discovered the magic of writing
poetry when she was a child. Poetry has always been a
kind of refuge for her. "Beautiful metaphors have often
healed me, where aspirin failed," says Anne. Besides
writing poetry, Anne paints abstract watercolors, runs a
small gardening business, and makes jewelry. Sylvan
walks bring her peace and inspiration.

ACKNOWLEDGMENTS

The poems noted herein first appeared in the
following publications, to whose editors grateful
acknowlegment is made: *Waterways* ("Things
Seen on the Trail", "Sestina for Muhamed Isa",
"Madsong and Headache", and "Song of Autumn
in Vermont") and *Blueline* ("June on Whiteface").
Poems on pages 11, 42, 53, 63, 68, 70, 82, 89. 99,
115, 134, 140, 155, and 159 are copyright ©
2000 by Betty Edelman. Drawings on pages 3, 20,
116 and the cover, and poems on pages 5, 21, 37,
51, 66, 100, 117, 124, 149, and 156 are copyright
© 2000 by Bruce Hesselbach. Drawings on
pages 16, 18, 26, 29, 39, 41, 52, 56, 61, 80, 83, 84,
85, 90, 91, 93, 96, 98, 113, 142, and 155 and poems
on pages 9, 16, 18, 27, 35, 40, 56, 83, 113, 121, 132,
143, 153, and 163 are copyright © 2000 by
Timothy Swaim Johnson. Poems on pages 15, 34,
43, 69, 71, 72, 77, 92, 95, 97, 126, 135, 146, and
158 are copyright © 2000 by Virginia Love.
Drawings on pages 10, 33, 45, 58, 127, and 137 and
poems on pages 10, 13, 19, 31, 33, 47, 55, 57, 58,
59, 64, 76, 81, 87, 90, 91, 114. 123, 129, 139, 141,
148, and162 are copyright © 2000 by Anne
Mausolff. Drawings on pages 24, 25, 32, 73, 78,
112, 119, 125, and 144 and poems on pages 8, 12,
14, 17, 24, 25, 32, 65, 75, 79, 85, 112, 118, 122,
125, 130, 133, 145, and 147 are copyright ©
2000 by Anne Yarosevich. The collection as a
whole is © 2000 by the Londonderry Poets. All
rights reserved. Reproductions in print or card
form of illustrations by Anne Mausolff are
available upon request to the publisher.